An Ekphrasis of Genesis

AN EKPHRASIS OF
GENESIS

a poet's musings

JOSEPH L. BENSINGER

Copyright © 2023 Joseph L. Bensinger

jben775@currently.com

ISBN 978-1-7377045-4-6

Edited and designed by Tell Tell Poetry

Printed in the United States of America

First Printing, 2023

For Twila, Jennifer, and Jesse—
who make me wiser every day.

CONTENTS

ACKNOWLEDGMENTS

To my wife, Twila, who helped to turn my scribbled notes and drafts into a shade of coherence, weaving a tapestry amongst my disparate thoughts—

To my children, Jennifer and Jesse, for their support—

And to Tell Tell Poetry, who made my manuscript intelligible and provided the encouragement to work through the grit of editing—

Thank you!

An Ekphrasis of Genesis

A thousand times ten thousand
stood the council of the One
in rapt attention to creation
and the voice that would become.

Powerful the multitude
that stood upon the throne
with praises soaring in amplitude
and joyful trumpets blown.

PROLOGUE

Genesis is a written history of who and what we are, and how we got here. It explains our associations with everything else we sense and interact with. Finally, it gives us a road map and travel guide by which we should govern our lives—the destination clear.

But there are those who have chosen to believe that they are the so-called "masters of the universe"—that they control everything, that they are the smartest and most powerful of creatures in creation, and that they actually can control their own destiny. But their ignorance cannot save them. Their refusal to search for truths beyond their own self-interests has been a characteristic of human beings since the beginning. They trip, fall, and fail because of their limited wisdom.

For human beings do have limited wisdom. They were not made to be all-knowing and all-seeing—that is someone else's job. And that someone is the spiritual father who gave rise to our making and loves us as His created children— at least you should hope so. Much of the public is highly skeptical of anything to do with the mystical aspect of life. It is understandable, considering many of the expounders and prognosticators who have spoken about it over the centuries. Another part of it—and the biggest part—is the ignorance that prevails. Ignorance breeds skepticism in otherwise intelligent people. It also breeds fear.

I have not yet written about the more mystical aspects of the development of humanity, although I have pondered upon and considered the important lessons to be learned because of these interactions. Should humankind find grace, it would only be because we understand the plan of development and the human

3

errors of the past that helped mold it. In my poetry here, I have highlighted some actions in Genesis as I have studied and reflected upon their significance. If nothing else, I hope the result at least inspires you to consider those passages in greater depth. Whether you agree or disagree with my thoughts, I hope this exercise leads to a deeper and more meaningful understanding of scripture.

The stage is set, the props complete, and Yahweh reacts to the actor's performance. The outline of the script is born and shall not be torn asunder.

May Yahweh forgive me my errors.

THE POSSIBLE

In the beginning there were only probabilities.
The universe could only come into existence if someone observed it.
It does not matter that the observers turned up several billion years later.
The universe exists because we are aware of it.

—Martin Rees, cosmologist and astrophysicist

And His light created a field
out of nothingness.
And His energy filled the void
with a somethingness.

And some of His energy
He condensed
into molecules of matter—

that being a solid form
with which He filled
the somethingness
and created the universe.

And God said, "Let there be . . ."
—and all was created. Through speech,
we are aware of His consciousness,
for it is a symbolic packaging of this.

And as He spoke, the matrix
of our reality was mapped.
And God saw that it was good.

For order was created
from the collapsing of possibilities
into a formed thought, a singularity.
That which is good is ordered.

And what is love but the creation
and maintenance of order,
the caring for something outside of self?

STAR DUST AND HYDROGEN

The Big Bang of promise creates time and space.
In the infinity of nothingness comes the Creator's face.
In six Earth days, the Artisan seeks to remold
a universe already many billions of years old.

The cosmic tears of love's kind heart,
which flow in unending wavelet art
and reconfigure the matter of the preceding blast,
provide the foothold of something more vast.

The planets and the stars become the clay
of firm creation and the kiln-fired day.
And Earth was sculpted on the Potter's wheels
with an objective of purpose this soon reveals.

A gas lantern was set to light up the sky
and the Earth was spun as a top on the fly.
And the water and salts—the life-giving pot—
were stirred in the mists with an elemental lot.

Bedded was the blue heavens' constant flow
between the water above and the water below
that recycled this nutrient, so widely broadcast,
over the rock and the rubble that had been amassed.

And the pyramid of life was built at long last.
The threads of the future of consciousness cast.
Now the Master must knead the impurities grown
to strengthen what the spindle of life has thrown.

THE TEMPLATE

Genesis 2:4–3:24

Together they were and together they stand—
the helper and the hand. Pondering the tree
of evil, against the Maker's command
—and bitter was the penalty and heavy the fee.

Access to the tree of eternal life was lost
and gained were the grind and labor of living.
A boundary was crossed and a path embossed,
which engendered in the future a redemptive giving.

First, a consciousness of the collective endears,
thus allowing them to see with one mind.
But then the freedom of will commandeers
and breaks down those strong ties that bind.

Like the small child, they knew togetherness
between themselves and the Master's mind.
A shared intimacy of profound connectedness
were now individuals with individual designs.

A road was taken for individual divisiveness
of the political standards for right and wrong
—truth mired in empowered self-righteousness
and suffocated in self-admiration's wild singsong.

Now imperfect beings in an imperfect world
with only a glimmer of the perfection that could be
—as the Garden of Eden from which two were hurled,
the hot sword of justice might never set free.

No plea to remedy the perpetual ban—
left to our whims and the fallen angel's voice,
with God's guidance in an overall plan
to allow us free will and the power of choice.

This is the error that over centuries we brace—
that, in arrogant belief, our wisdom is strong
enough to be shepherds to the Earth we debase
when we are in misery with the ills we prolong—

in an unfinished world out of Eden's domain,
in a place we have created out of hardship and pain,
where illness begets us and corruption does reign
and accidents of imperfectness add to the strain.

PROTEVANGELIUM

Genesis 3:1–3:24

Long-lasting, the battle betwixt woman and dragon
as a boundary was breached and a curse unchained.
For it entailed a rebellion that swallowed keen passion.
And all that was given was not what was gained.

And the Eve of humanity was just as conceived—
a helper to Adam in duplicity's scheme,
a predictable in the Master's tapestry weaved,
a law that was broken and would tear the seam.

With Adam, an heir to the grace of life—
bone of my bones and flesh of my flesh—
fallen as angels to the earth of dire strife.
The cost of free will and foolishness, fresh.

Naked with shame, but no sign of regret.
No shadow of guilt did they beget.
No fear did they show that for sin there'd be debt.
No synergy, nor unity—all lost on a bet.

The story continues of the shames that entomb us
in breaking the laws that make for our oneness.
We bury our actions in grief that consumes us,
that deepens the evil that makes for our numbness.

Sometime in the future when generations have passed,
a daughter of Eve will bear the blessed seed
and the grace of forgiveness for all sins amassed,
for those who repent of misguided misdeed.

RAISING CAIN

Genesis 4:1–4:16 and Luther's Works 1:242

Not the promised savior, as Eve would believe,
his righteousness in question as sin would take seed
and plant the wrath from which he would later grieve,
in a conscious growth before the incurable bleed.

Persistent true faith, not in good works as shown,
but in the plow of the field where the sweet fruit grows.
Not the ground that lies fallow where nothing is sown,
but the continual tilling that abundance well-knows.

Of dark hidden views that unspoken deceive
comes the one who would lie in anger and dismay.
The staining blood of the brother the field would receive
and the richness of good earth would harden to clay.

Upright integrity, not watered devotion,
would have led to a finer crop of promotion.

SUBMERGED

Flocking to their own authority as before,
gulled by the sons of God and their spawn,
their mores as flighty as feathers that soar
in corruption so nested that attention was drawn.

In action and deed and the flight of their thought
as hunkered in the imaginings of human hearts,
fornication, violence, and crime were wrought
and the evil of injustice winged all manner of arts.

Monsters of perversion—none would be staying.
No perch above waters—He would condemn.
With deep sadness of heart, the Lord was heard saying
in earnest: *I repent that I made them.*

Found rebelling entirely against the Almighty's love,
all souls doomed but for the mercy of the dove.

THE TOWER OF BABEL.

THE CLIMB TO BABBLE

Genesis 11:1–11:9

A lofty but ponderous tower that will scale the sky,
reaching the heavens with bitumen binding and brick
in a brash and haughty boast to match the Most High—
douse the holy candle and dislodge the wick.

As descendants of Noah, humanity spoke in one tongue.
To become mighty in strength and united in name,
amongst all the peoples Nimrod's glory was sung.
And all the known world idol-worshipped the fame.

As the city grew, so did arrogance and vainglorious pride.
The makers of wood and stone gods were fast-peddling
to oil the faithfuls' lamp and illuminate their stride.
But the flame of wrath shall unleash the winds of reckoning.

They imagined in their hearts to war against the One
and so His house in the nation of Abraham was begun.

CAST YOUR LOT

Genesis 18:16–19:29

The outcry was great against the actions of the accused.
Mistreatment of travelers—a great evil endured.
Strangers were used, mistreated, and cruelly abused.
No survival on a road without hospitality secured.

Yahweh in the flesh, the judge of the world, arrived
to see for Himself the cause of such clamor and commotion.
Though His judgment is patient for the weak and deprived,
it became evident this required the first law of motion.

And harm was spewed as a quake shook the foundation,
with gases, brimstone, and burning bitumen in flight.
A rift in the earth bends the land to prostration
that ends in a Dead Sea of nothing—a salted gravesite.

The behavior of the wicked cries out for condemnation,
and the care for the vulnerable requires divine disposition.

THE GUIDEPOST

Genesis 20:1–22:19

His seed becomes the resounding reed of the Redeemer,
for he chose to be a servant in obedience to the Lord
and roundly rejected the idolatrous altars of Ur.
To his successors in spirit and body—the blessed chord.

Yet his utter everlasting belief in Yahweh would slip,
for his sacred trust was blurred in promises he'd heard.
But faith can be fostered through trial and hardship
to reach salvation by virtue of trust in His word.

Though lacking in wisdom, we aren't absolved of sin,
but Yahweh takes human shortcoming into account.
It's not works but Yahweh's kindness that weighs in.
God is faithful in His promises—free will can't discount.

Free will shall not smudge the blueprint of His plan.
He conditions the situation of the choices of man.

ISAAC BLESSING JACOB.

THE TRICKSTER

Genesis 25:19–25:34

And the younger held on to the foot of the older,
perhaps an attempt to juggle their position at birth.
For the first-born son becomes the paternal beholder
of the blessings of power and familial worth.

Esau becomes footloose and marries two daughters
of the idol-worshippers who live in the land of Canaan.
Of a wild nature, he generally walked in rough waters,
unperturbed with the beliefs and prided marches of the pagan.

A bowl of soup and a bold mimic of his sibling
gained the younger brother his father's blessing.
But for all the footrace in the family scribbling,
God's favor is not an upshot of human pressing.

Covenantal fulfillment is mighty God's aim.
So, by grace, an heir and Israel shall be his name.

PAYBACK

Genesis 28:10–31:55

And his father's desire to richly bless the older
will not sway the fibers of providence of the Lord,
but only harkens a hardship upon the beholder,
as sturdy hands will make for a stronger cord.

And Jacob's deceit was served upon himself
and tested his patience and strengthened his resolve,
his mask a reflection of the mirror upon the shelf
of an image of darkness where wisdom must evolve.

The Lord gives us the gifts of logic and will
and waits for us to do for ourselves when possible—
His gifts not to be neglected but used in goodwill.
But the caring Lord's plan will suffer no obstacle.

Through God's blessing and grace came a clear heading
for Jacob's confident stride and firm treading.

DEVOTION

Genesis 32:1–32:31

Yahweh's script for redemption plays out,
along with His covenant promises of blessing,
even though casts of imperfect actors sprout
and smother lives with acts that are distressing.

Abraham's seed, through Isaac, wrestled with God—
struggling in character, slowly shifting in attitude.
Yet always in blessing and good graces he trod,
as his soundness, integrity, and wisdom accrued.

Though humans fail to triumph over sin—
forever treading in a dank, loose-footed mire,
staging sorrow in the gracious Creator therein—
unwavering faith can overcome Yahweh's ire.

He struggled with faith that Yahweh's will would prevail
and chose first to stumble along his own ponderous trail.

THE HELPER

Genesis 37:2–37:36, 39:1–50:26

His steadfast faithfulness well-endured all his life
through envy, deceit, confinement, and huge success,
because a righteous lifestyle dulls the knife
of evil such that the Lord's grace will finesse.

From son to slave to conscript to pharaoh's man,
neither misfortune nor enticement would slice or stave
Joseph's wisdom or God's providential plan,
for his trusting humility knots the grace God gave.

The trials and tribulations are raveled and awry
for those who would distrust or try the Lord.
His plan to splice the cord and secure the tie
begets a braided journey yet to be explored.

In the woven trail of Moses, the seed will transplant
in the final fulfillment of Abram's covenantal grant.

PROMISES

the Book of Genesis

God finally orphaned those idolatrous nations
that slowly grew after the worldwide purging flood,
and found in the families of Abraham foundations
for covenants that would drain the Dragon's blood.

The cloak of wrath will be trimmed in mercy's lace
by a change in the Master's fashion of teaching,
creating a holy harmonious shroud of grace
revealed in the salvation of the undeserving.

The shroud of one who will release us from sin—
the bloody redeeming shroud that was yet to come
from out of the wasteland of self-destroying din
with a final new promise and a passionate drum.

The trumpet's salvation in the orchestra of provenance
is for humans who seek the ring of resonant consonance.

SEEKING GRACE

Before the acknowledged fruit
—the apple of decision—
God was responsible for us.
With free will, to choose between
lovingkindness and wickedness,
we became responsible for ourselves.

With the weight of the Sacrifice,
we are forgiven our foolish choices
and redeemed of our misdeeds
so as to provide a clear path
to needed and necessary learning.

For all our earthly choices,
for those who will listen
to the prolific lessons of life,
provide training in awareness
of what we might forethink
to hear, acknowledge, and act on.

NOTES

"**The Possible**": In this poem, there are two excerpts that are borrowed from the Holy Bible (ESV). "And God said, 'Let there be . . .'" comes from Genesis 1:3, 1:6, and 1:14. "And God saw that it was good . . ." comes from Genesis 1:10, 1:12, 1:18, 1:21, and 1:25.

"**The Template**": This poem follows the events of Genesis 2:4–3:24. To elaborate on the last line of this poem: Accidents that occur in an imperfect world add to the strain of misery. But in a perfect world, there are no accidents.

"**Protevangelium**": This poem follows the events of Genesis 3:1–3:24. There is also an excerpt in this poem that is borrowed from the Holy Bible (ESV). "[B]one of my bones and flesh of my flesh . . ." comes from Genesis 2:23.

"**Raising Cain**": This poem follows the events of Genesis 4:1–4:16 and *Luther's Works* (242). In the last line of this poem, "promotion" refers to being in favor of God. As stated in Genesis 4:5: ". . . but for Cain and his offering [crop] he had no regard" (ESV).

"**Submerged**": This poem follows the events of Genesis 6–8. There is also an excerpt in this poem that is borrowed from *The Complete Apocrypha: With Enoch, Jasher, and Jubilees* (LSV). "I repent that I made them . . ." comes from Jasher 4:19 (LSV 300). For further reference and context in regards to this poem:

> • And Yahweh said, "I will never again curse the ground . . . [nor] . . . strike down every living creature . . . found" (ESV, Genesis 8:21).

"The Climb to Babble": This poem follows the events of Genesis 11:1–11:9. For further reference and context in regards to this poem:

> • And so "... they imagined in their hearts to war against him and to ascend into heaven"—but their destiny was dim (LSV 307, Jasher 9:25).

"Cast Your Lot": This poem follows the events of Genesis 18:16–19:29. The "first law of motion" here refers to the scientific principle of the same name penned by Sir Isaac Newton: that "a body remains in the state of rest or uniform motion in a straight line unless and until an external force acts on it." For further reference and context in regards to this poem:

> • "... [T]he smoke of the land went up like the smoke of a furnace" (ESV, Genesis 19:28). And so, the land was cleansed of unhealthy impureness.

"The Guidepost": This poem follows the events of Genesis 20:1–22:19. For further reference and context in regards to this poem:

> • "But God came to Abimelech in a dream by night and said to him, 'Behold, you are a dead man because of the woman ...'" (ESV, Genesis 20:3).

> • Jesus said, "Your father Abraham rejoiced that he would see my day. He saw it and was glad" (ESV, John 8:56).

"The Trickster": This poem follows the events of Genesis 25:19–25:34. For further reference and context in regards to this poem:

> • "... the older shall serve the younger" (ESV, Genesis 25:23).

> • And Abraham said: "... let them [your sons] not take to themselves wives from the daughters of Canaan; for the seed of Canaan will be rooted out of the land" (LSV 261, Jubilees 20:4).

- "And may He cleanse you [Jacob] from all un-righteousness and impurity, that you may be forgiven all (thy) transgressions; (and) your sins of ignorance" (LSV 264, Jubilees 22:14).

"Payback": This poem follows the events of Genesis 28:10–31:55. For further reference and context in regards to this poem:

- "For I [Abraham] know that the Lord will choose him to be a people (nation) for possession unto Himself, above all peoples that are upon the face of the earth" (LSV 261, Jubilees 19:18).

"Devotion": This poem follows the events of Genesis 32:1–32:31. For further reference and context in regards to this poem:

- ". . . I [Jacob] am not worthy of the least of all the deeds of steadfast love and all the faithfulness that you have shown to your servant . . ." (ESV, Genesis 32:10).

- "Your name shall no longer be called Jacob, but Israel, for you have striven with God and with men, and have prevailed" (ESV, Genesis 32:28).

"The Helper": This poem follows the events of Genesis 37:2–37:36 and 39:1–50:26. For further reference and context in regards to this poem:

- "As for you, you meant evil against me [Joseph], but God meant it for good, to bring it about that many people should be kept alive, as they are today" (ESV, Genesis 50:20).

- ". . . I [Joseph] am about to die, but God will visit you and bring you up out of this land [Egypt] to the land that he swore to Abraham, to Isaac, and to Jacob" (ESV, Genesis 50:24).

"Promises": This poem follows the events of the full book of Genesis. Concerning the homecoming achieved in Exodus and the fulfillment of the covenant, the satirical comment by Michael S. Heiser seems appropriate here: "What could go wrong?" (TUR 180).

"Seeking Grace": This poem was previously published as "School's in Session" in the collection: *Beginnings and Ends: Poetry of Man, Nature, and Human Thought*, by Joseph L. Bensinger. Second Edition, 2022.

REFERENCES

Arnold, Bill T. and Bryan E. Beyer. *Encountering the Old Testament: A Christian Survey*. Third Edition. Grand Rapids: Baker Academic, 2015.

Berlin, Adele and Marc Zvi Brettler (editors). *The Jewish Study Bible*. Second Edition. New York: Oxford University Press, 2014. (Tanakh)

Covenant Christian Coalition. *The Complete Apocrypha: With Enoch, Jasher, and Jubilees*. 2018 Edition. New York: Covenant House, 2018.

Engelbrecht, Rev. Edward A. (editor). *The Lutheran Study Bible: English Standard Version*. St. Louis: Concordia Publishing House, 2009. (ESV)

Heiser, Michael S. *The Unseen Realm: Recovering the Supernatural Worldview of the Bible*. Bellingham: Lexham Press, 2015.

Lanza, Robert and Matej Pavšič, Bob Berman. *The Grand Biocentric Design: How Life Creates Reality*. Dallas: BenBella Books, 2021.

Luther, Martin. *Luther's Works, Volume 1: Lectures on Genesis Chapters 1-5*. American Edition. St. Louis: Concordia Publishing House, 1958.

North, Jason. *Creation of Species: The Role of Angels in Intelligent Design*. Las Vegas: Jason North, 2022.

Thagard, Christian. *Earth Game: The Evolution of Consciousness*. Orlando: Christian Thagard, 2022.

Watkin, Christopher. *Thinking Through Creation: Genesis 1 and 2 as Tools of Cultural Critique*. Phillipsberg: P&R Publishing Company, 2017.

Yee, Gale A. and Hugh R. Page Jr., Matthew J. M. Coomber (editors). *Fortress Commentary on the Bible: The Old Testament and Apocrypha*. Minneapolis: Fortress Press, 2014.

ABOUT THE AUTHOR

Joseph L. Bensinger is the author of four previous poetry collections: *Man, Ships, and the Sea*; *Of Curses and Blessings*; *Journeys through the Tapestry*; and *Beginnings and Ends*. His poems have appeared in *Haiku Journal*, *WestWard Quarterly*, *Ocean Magazine*, and *Mobius*. Before retiring, he worked as an electronics project engineer, a computer systems manager, and a teaching anthropologist. He now spends his time writing ethnohistory and poetry.

Printed in Great Britain
by Amazon

24690341R00034